TOP TIPS:
REACHING UNCHURCHED CHILDREN

Helen Franklin

Copyright © 2005
First published 2005
Reprinted 2009
ISBN 978 1 84427 127 6

Scripture Union, 207–209 Queensway,
Bletchley, Milton Keynes, MK2 2EB,
England
Email: info@scriptureunion.org.uk
Website: www.scriptureunion.org.uk

Scripture Union Australia
Locked Bag 2, Central Coast Business
Centre, NSW 2252
Website: www.scriptureunion.org.au

Scripture Union USA
PO Box 987,Valley Forge, PA 19482
Website: www.scriptureunion.org

British Library Cataloguing-in-
Publication Data.
A catalogue record of this book is
available from the British Library.

Printed and bound in Singapore by
Tien Wah Press Ltd

Logo and cover design:
www.splash-design.co.uk

Internal design:
www.splash-design.co.uk

Internal illustrations:
Colin Smithson

Scripture Union is an
international Christian charity working
with churches in more than 130
countries, providing resources to bring
the good news about Jesus Christ to
children, young people and families
and to encourage them to develop
spiritually through the Bible and
prayer.

As well as our network of volunteers,
staff and associates who run holidays,
church-based events and school
Christian groups, we produce a wide
range of publications and support
those who use our resources through
training programmes.

INTRODUCTION

Liam was seven years old. It was his first time at 'Tuesday Club', the weekly Christian club run by local churches at his school, where he was asked a question about God. 'I don't know anything about God,' said Liam, 'except my Dad says he made the world.'

Liam is not unusual; you probably know a lot of similar children. Like most children today he has no experience of church, no relative who reads the Bible and no knowledge of God except the barest of facts.

So where do we begin and how do we talk about Jesus with children like Liam who know so little? And where do we start with those who have never even been told that God made the world? In this book we will look at some of the problems and the Biblical principles behind talking about Jesus with those who know nothing about him. We shall consider some practical possibilities for helping children who are unconnected with a church community to catch sight of Jesus.

When I am decorating my house, I can never wait for the moment when I load the brush with paint and put the new colour on the wall. I am so eager that I often rush the preparation stages in my haste to get into the paint tin! Parts 1 and 2 of this book may seem like the work that has to be done before painting can begin, but thinking through these things will make your work with children so much more effective.

As you read, keep in mind the children with whom God brings you into contact, their lives, the things that take up their time and interest and where all that fits with what you read. Ask God to make you more effective in helping them to know Jesus. And ask yourself this question: If nobody had ever told you about Jesus, what would you miss the most? It is part of your motivation for helping children to know Jesus.

SOME OF THE CHALLENGES

1 Contact

When, where and how do we meet children today? Gone are the days when large numbers of children were sent to church by their parents every week. The majority of children in church on a Sunday are there with their parents, so the number of children connected with church is relatively small. Back in 1991, it was less than one in seven and it has been declining ever since. Liam has never gone to church on a Sunday. If we are to help other children to know about Jesus and to come to know him, we will have to go outside church to meet them. We will have to think beyond Sunday as the best time to work with children.

When?
For people who do not go to church, Sunday is often prime time for
- leisure
- shopping
- sport
- visiting relatives who live a distance away
- travel
- access to children by parents who do not live with them

Sunday is a busy day for many families. We will have more chance of attracting children to activities on a different day. Instead of bemoaning falling numbers in churches, find new times to run children's work and new ways to make what we do more attractive to those with no church background. Increasing numbers of churches are running midweek clubs. These are proving successful in helping them to meet children with no ties to a church. We shall look at these in more detail in Part 3.

Where?

Liam is in school Mondays to Fridays. He is familiar with it and although it is primarily a place of learning for him, it is a short walk from home and it is a place where he feels comfortable. We may have more success running activities on what children see as their territory – perhaps in their local school or some other community building. They may be more likely to come to our event if they are familiar with the place where it is held. In Part 3 we shall look at potential opportunities in schools, both formally as part of the school day and informally as a venue for an after-school club.

Do we need an indoor venue for children's work? Not always! It may be that we can run a club outside, where we can be seen by anyone. The possibilities will be limited by the weather, but a club held on a village green, in a local park or on waste ground in a city suburb may be very effective. We cannot just walk up to children and start talking to them in the street. If we are making friendships in more informal settings then we ought to be sure that we introduce ourselves to parents or carers too, so that they know who we are and what we are doing. We need the backing of a local church for what we do, so that there are accountability structures and so that adults working with

In reality…

Scripture Union in French-speaking Switzerland runs clubs that they call 'Bar-Jack' – the name is a colloquialism for 'bar chat' and reflects the informal nature of the club. They set up a 'bar' (covered table!) in a prominent place in the community and the club meets there every week for chat, games and Bible-based activities.

children are properly checked, in line with current legislation. There are problems to be overcome, but don't let a lack of venue put you off!

Who?

Although it is highly probable that you are reading this book alone, you should not be working alone with children. However deep our concern for children to hear about Jesus, we do need to work to the standards that current legislation demands. It is for everyone's safety – the children's and yours, for the peace of mind of parents, for the reputation of our work and ultimately of Jesus himself. In purely practical terms it is vital in case of an accident, but it is a measure of our care for children that we work to recognised standards. So as you read on, keep thinking in terms of what 'you' (plural) – a church or team of children's workers – can do.

Make sure that you carry out thorough checks to the required standards on everyone who works with children, or who is using the building at the same time as any children's groups meet. For more information check with either your denominational children's work department or contact The Churches' Child Protection Advisory Service (CCPAS) at PO Box 133, Swanley, Kent, BR8 7UQ (0845 120 550) or www.ccpas.co.uk

2 Spirituality

After the birth of his first son, Brooklyn, David Beckham said, 'I definitely want Brooklyn to be christened, but I don't know into what religion yet.' That comment suggests that a) he has failed to realise that 'christening' relates only to Christianity and b) he has no clear religious beliefs. That is not a criticism, just an example of the way that many people think today. They appear to be graduates from the 'Heinz

School of Theology'. Although they may not have the full 57 varieties of beliefs, what they believe will probably come from a wide range of sources, a variety of religions and folklore. Traditional Christian thinking may not feature.

At the same time, however, people are much more open to spiritual things. 'Spirituality' is a buzzword in school and children are encouraged to be reflective. Rather than seeing it as a threat we need to make the most of this opportunity. In Part 2 we'll look at how the apostle Paul coped with the mix of beliefs that he found among the people of Athens.

Of course in multicultural Britain, we are likely to meet children from strong, but not Christian, faith backgrounds. We need to understand something of their culture and faith so that we can welcome them and share the love of Jesus without pressure to change their beliefs. A person from another faith who converts to Christianity could face opposition from their family, and we must be aware of this. Someone experienced in working with children from other faith backgrounds says, 'We can give them the opportunity to explore in a simple way what the Bible says. The challenge then comes from the working of the Holy Spirit in their lives through what is studied, and not from the leaders.'

3 Assumptions

In today's spiritual climate, there may be no common understanding of what we mean when we talk about God or Jesus. So we can make no assumptions about the knowledge children have. We need to think about things from their perspective, to explain basic truths and to tell basic Bible stories, rather than expecting them to have heard them before. In a school staff-room I once saw a list on the wall headed 'Bible Roundabout'. Conversation with a teacher revealed that none of the staff knew any Bible stories so each had learned one story, and then taught it in turn to every class.

This has all kinds of practical implications for our work, from avoiding quiz questions that need Bible knowledge other than what has been given that day, to explaining how to find books, chapters and verses in the Bible using the index. We cannot make sweeping statements such as, 'We all believe that…', and we may find ourselves with the awesome responsibility of being the first to tell children what has happened because Jesus died on the cross!

We should also make no assumptions about a child's family

background – whether or not they live with both parents or whether the people who care for them have the same surname. Discover, remember and use the right titles, in letters home and in our choice of words. Whether speaking to that child or all the group use expressions such as, 'Tell your grown-ups at home…'

4 Language and ideas

A colleague tells of a child in school who put up her hand during an RE lesson and said, 'Miss, there's a swear word on this worksheet. It says "Jesus"!'

What words do you use when the chance comes to explain the Bible's message to a child? As with avoiding assumptions, we need to work at a basic level. It can be a great challenge to explain Biblical or Christian 'jargon' words such as 'grace', 'mercy', and 'salvation' in everyday language, but it is an important skill to develop. How do we explain some of the ideas that are central to the Christian message? We shall look at this again in Part 3.

5 Integration to church

Think about...

Using everyday language and ideas that a child of ten would understand, write an explanation of what it means to be a Christian.

Here is a key question to ask before we start: What will we do if these children come to church? They may behave in ways that are unacceptable to the rest of the congregation such as talking, asking questions or running round after the service. But look at it from the other perspective. These children may not know what any of it means, but they want the warmth and love of a caring community and we ought to be able to offer that. So in what ways do we need to be different and to 'do church' differently? This is a question for the whole church but they may look to you for a lead on it.

If the children and their families begin to come to church, it will make a difference to what happens in services. Otherwise they are likely to walk away because they do not understand, are unable to cope or are not made to feel welcome. There is a relevant article called 'Have I got church for you?' on the Scripture Union eye level website: www.scriptureunion.org.uk/eyelevel

These are just some of the challenges that we face as we help children who are unconnected with church to know Jesus. How you respond to each will depend on you, your situation, and the children that you are reaching with the love of Jesus.

2

THE BIBLICAL PRINCIPLES (ACTS 17:16–34)

A journey to Athens in Acts 17:16–34, to see how Paul fared in that city among people of a different spiritual understanding, will help us to find some Biblical principles for our evangelism. Read the verses now before going further.

Of course we cannot draw total parallels between what we are doing and what happened then, not least because Paul was talking with adults, and very learned adults at that. But there are some important things to notice that will inspire us.

Think about…

What things in the children's lives distress you? List them here and ask God to show you how to react to them.

- Paul was in Athens. Where has God put you? Or where is God calling you to be? Paul was in Athens – he was a 'missionary' abroad, but you are just as much a missionary if you are taking the good news of Jesus to people in your own community.

- Paul was **distressed by the Athenians' devotion to idols** (verse 16).
Do the things that dominate children's lives cause us to be concerned for them? Do we care about the influences on them and the 'idols' that are held up before them? How can you find out more about these influences? Do you watch what they watch, listen to what they listen to, get excited by their teams, read what they read, know what toys are in fashion, know what makes them insecure, fearful, hopeful or hopeless? That takes time and effort on your part!

- Paul was **out and about where the people were**; not just debating among the faith community but talking with ordinary people in the market place (verse 17).

Few children come to church on their own, or even with parents, unless they are Christians or are at least sympathetic to the Christian message. To make new contacts we need to be active in our local communities.

- Paul found **people who were thinkers** (verses 18–21). The Stoics and Epicureans may not have shared Paul's beliefs but they were debaters who loved to think about things.

What was it in Paul's message that set the Stoics and Epicureans thinking? He was preaching the good news about Jesus and his resurrection. It may be inappropriate for us to jump in with the cross and resurrection but it is an essential piece of the Christian message that we need to teach at some stage. We too, need to be thinkers so that we can explain the deepest of truths in everyday language, ideas and concepts.

There are children today who ask big questions and who think deeply. Even when a child is completely unconnected with church, we are not speaking into a spiritual vacuum. God has been here before. If

In reality…

Jamie was six when I met him at a holiday club. He had never been to church before but the church's community worker who lived down his road had invited him. Jamie was fostered by his aunt, who was the local drug pusher. Day after day at the holiday club Jamie heard the story of the apostle Peter. He was riveted by it. Midweek, we came to the account of Peter and John at the Beautiful Gate on their way to the temple, when a beggar asked them for money. Suddenly Jamie jumped up from his seat and came and stood in front of me, his eyes shining brightly. 'And then Jesus healed the man!' he said, with total understanding and great excitement.

only we will look for his footprints.

• **Recognition of common ground** (verse 22).
In the case of Paul and the Athenians, the common ground was their interest in religion. They wanted to know more and Paul had lots to tell them!

It is unlikely to be 'religion' with children today, so what do we have in common? It may be football, music, astronomy, cooking or a love of nature. Whatever it is, we can use it as a way to develop a friendship and, in time, to talk about Jesus.

• **They took Paul to the Areopagus**, the city's meeting place for debate and discussion (verse 19).
How do we know when we are 'in' with children? It is when they bring their friends to our group or club. We need to make our clubs and events places where they want to bring their friends.

• At the Areopagus Paul picked up on the fact they had dedicated an altar 'to an unknown God' (verse 23). It was a sign that they wanted to cover all eventualities and not miss a deity 'off their list', but Paul used it as a starting point for talking about Jesus. Then he began to **fill in the missing details in their knowledge**.

- How did Paul talk about God? He used **common, everyday language** (verses 24–31). He taught them about the deep things of God in the simplest of words.

Do you remember Liam, who featured in the introduction? The Liams that we meet need us to talk

Think about...

Shared interests.
What are the interests you and the children share? What points of connection do you have?

their language. Christian jargon that uses words like sin, grace, salvation, is the language of a specific group of people and is therefore exclusive. We must use everyday words and ideas that can be understood by anyone no matter how long they have been part of that group.

- Paul told the Athenians a vital truth early on: **God wanted people** to seek him, to reach out and to find him (verse 27).

This is a great truth to impart to children as they make their first contacts with Christians and with church! Many children have an image of God as someone who makes the rules, who stops them having fun and who is an old man, out of touch with their lives. In reality, God loves and wants them as his friends.

- Paul gave a very simple explanation of God's work and **applied it to his hearers** (verses 30, 31).

- There is little reference to Jesus in this passage. Instead of saying everything he knew straight away, Paul **went back and talked again** (verse 32).

We need a long-term view of evangelism with children who are not used to church. We do not have to tell them everything in one session, even if it may be the only time that we meet them. They will simply not take it in.

We should never manipulate anyone into making a hasty, unreasonable response to Jesus. That is especially so with children. Their natural reaction is to say 'Yes' if you ask them if they want to follow Jesus. They probably want to please you. Our work needs the hallmark of integrity that allows time to think and consider what it means, so that when they say 'Yes' to Jesus, they mean it. That is especially so with children who are not used to church.

God will be at work in children long after we have met them. While we should never be lazy in our evangelism, neither should we force-feed everything in our haste to make up lost time, nor force decisions about following Jesus.

Keep these things in mind as you work with children who have not previously had experience of church. But now, to go back to my decorating metaphor, let's pick up the paintbrush and open the tin!

PRACTICAL POSSIBILITIES

3

School

School is the place where all children have to be! It is a prime place to meet children who do not connect with church, although its prime purpose is education. We need to tread carefully if we are going to work here, but there are so many opportunities available! The place to start is with the head teacher, either asking if you might run a Christian group, or simply asking what help the school needs, and then meeting that need.

A former schools' worker with Scripture Union, always said that if a church wanted an opening into their local school they should start by offering to wash the paint pots on a regular basis! It might not offer much contact with children initially but it might open doors for the future. One minister decided to become a dinnertime supervisor to give him ample opportunity to build appropriate relationships with the children.

In all of this we must have integrity. Our primary reason for being there is to meet a need in the school.

Assemblies

We must respect the educational context of an assembly and remember that children have not chosen to be here. This is not the time or place for an appeal for children to follow Jesus, but is an opportunity to explain more about 'what the Bible says' or 'what Christians believe', to use two common phrases that make our comments acceptable. Although we may feel that it gives us little contact with individual children, they will see and become familiar with us. Assemblies can be a great way to meet local children. There are a number of resources with ideas. Visit the Scripture Union website for details of the SU ones – www.scriptureunion. org.uk/resources

RE Lessons

If you are inexperienced in school the idea of taking an RE lesson may seem daunting, but these too are great opportunities to talk with children. Check with a teacher as to what is appropriate in terms of content, style and methods. There are a number of resources available to help. Remember that the children are there to be educated. It is different from a club where they come by choice.

Clubs

A Christian club could be run at lunchtime or after school. It would have to fit around the school timetable and would need to be very flexible, very simple and probably very short. For ideas of how to set up and run a club in a Primary school, and information about materials and resources, see www.scriptureunion.org.uk/schools

Visits

Increasing numbers of churches are creating opportunities to work with schools at specific times of the year.

• Many churches welcome school visits as part of the RE curriculum. Some dress up children to take part in a 'wedding' while others take children round the building, explaining the significance of the font or baptistery, communion table or altar. There is a booklet about this, *Linking Churches and Schools*, published by Churches Together in England, available from 27 Tavistock Square, London WC1H 9HH (www.churches-together.org.uk).

• Many schools use their local church for carol services or harvest festivals. Make good use of the opportunity! Ask someone to greet children, staff and parents as they arrive. Display leaflets advertising clubs, groups or events for children, giving contact details, as well as times of special services for that festival. Make it a good experience for all who come. That makes it easier for them to come midweek or on a Sunday.

Gift books
A new opening into many schools and the lives of thousands of children has been through churches giving books to help the pupils at

particular times. Other RE resources are usually welcomed as gifts.

• *It's Your Move* (Scripture Union) helps Year 6 pupils move on to secondary school. See www.scriptureunion.org.uk/itsyourmove for more details.

• *Get Ready, Go!* is a book for young children starting school. It includes a booklet for parents too.

Church

Much of what we do through church will be long-term evangelism, building up friendships and often showing Jesus before we speak about him.

Churches tend to have a 'fringe' of people who come to events where they might hear the message of Jesus. There will probably also be children and their families whose only contact with church is the club or group that meets on church premises. We need to develop these contacts as much as possible. Many of the following ideas are more about contact with families than just contact with children, but that is very important. If we draw in parents, we will reach their children too.

Parent and toddler groups, pram services, parenting courses etc

If it is a church-run group it may help to have someone on the team whose main task is to get to know parents, invite them to other events or activities and have a pastoral role. If the group simply meets on church premises but is run by others, try to get someone from church to work on the team. My 80-year-old mother is 'Monday's Granny' and reads stories to children who need a bit of space and quiet. But she is also a link between the group and the church where the group meets. See the Tiddlywinks range of resources (Scripture Union), for these groups, www.scriptureunion.org.uk/resources

Uniformed organisations

These may not be your first thought when it comes to a strategy to reach unconnected children, but they often have excellent contact with children who do not come to Sunday activities. More than 60% of girls involved in the Girls' Brigade only have a connection with church through the Brigade.

Christingle and carol services

Christmas is probably the key time when families who would never normally come to church might consider coming. These services need to be user-friendly, making families feel welcome, using well-known carols, having a simple, non-threatening structure and offering the real 'magic' of Christmas. The words used should be ordinary and understandable. The services should be joyful and make them want to come back for more! For more ideas see *Christmas Wrapped Up* (Scripture Union).

Drama, music and all that jazz!

Several churches put on a pantomime at Christmas (the kind that have a dame, a lot of laughter and plenty of 'He's behind you!' from the audience). One church, wanting to involve members of the community, advertised in the local paper offering auditions. 120 people turned up! In another pantomime, the real-life wife of the 'dame' sold tickets to a family they knew through their son's rugby team. At the boys' training session a week later, the dad turned to her and said, 'So what is it that you believe?'

Special interest clubs

This covers all kinds of things – sport, drama, music, art, cookery – the list is endless! If you can run a club about anything that children want  to come to, you have an opening to tell them about Jesus. It may be that for a long time this 'telling' is done through who you are, not through what you say. Your main aim should be to run the best club possible of whatever kind it is. If you see it as just a way to make 'contacts' then it will probably fail. The children's reason for coming is to learn that skill, or develop their ability in that area, so you need to enable that to happen. If it is a sports club, get as many leaders as possible trained to be accredited coaches. If it is a drama or music club, make sure that those running it are experienced enough to run a good club. Make yours the best it can possibly be!

Links to adult evangelism

Many churches have effectively run Alpha, Discovering Christianity or Y Courses for adults. We may be able to link in with these opportunities and run events for the children of adults on the course, especially when parents attend daytime events. But what about a course for children who want to know more?

You can doubtless think of many other ways to make and develop contacts. The key thing is that we make the most of opportunities to get to know children, to chat with them and to build genuine friendships with them. But what next? How do we develop these and begin to talk more about Jesus?

Special events

One-off events such as Christmas or summer fun days are a good way to begin. To a large extent they rely on good contacts – either by leaders, or by children bringing their friends. A day at Christmas can do wonders for relationships with parents, allowing them time for Christmas shopping in peace! Invite them for refreshments at the end of the day, sing a couple of well-known carols and give a very short talk about Christmas. See *Christmas Wrapped Up* (Scripture Union) for ideas.

Holiday clubs

These are a great way to tell children about Jesus. Resources for them abound, and the Scripture Union books include tips for running a club.
Here are some 'top tips' to make the club more effective in attracting and welcoming unchurched children, rather than just your Sunday regulars.

- **Publicity**. Make it colourful and eye-catching with leaflets for individual children, and posters to put in local shops, schools, the library and swimming pool – and outside church too. If possible, take an assembly in the local school before the club begins.

In reality…

The holiday club at Christchurch Pennington was videoed, and all the children plus their families were invited back two weeks later to view the edited edition. During the evening families were invited to the harvest supper a few weeks later. At that event, tickets were on sale for a bonfire party four weeks ahead, and at the end of that evening people were invited to the Christmas party. And so it went on. At each event an invitation was offered to the next one. By the following summer the church had seen many of the children and their families several times throughout the year!

- **Entry**. Make it easy for children to come into the venue by putting coloured footprints to mark the route from the footpath to the door.

- **Songs**. Teach all as if new and explain their meaning, so that new children are not excluded. Avoid songs that include words that may not be true for some children, like 'I believe…' or 'I'm going to follow…'

- **Quizzes**. Include lots of general knowledge questions to build confidence among the children. If questions relate to Bible passages, make sure that they can be answered by anyone who has been there that day, not just children with previous Bible knowledge.

- **Bible verses**. Although there is value in simply learning Bible verses, it is even better if children understand what use the verse is. For example, in a holiday club on a sport theme, call it 'the coach quote'. Tell the children that a coach tells an athlete how to run a race. In the same way, the Bible helps us to do things God's way.

- **Parents**. Appoint someone to greet families as they arrive and chat to parents when they come to collect their children.

- **Plan** follow-on events in advance.

As well as follow-on events, where possible we need to offer regular clubs of a similar style to the holiday club - midweek or on Saturdays, weekly, fortnightly or monthly - but they need that same hallmark of fun, Bible-based activities and time that allows children and leaders to build friendships, or as a former colleague put it, 'To build bridges strong enough for Jesus to walk across.'

Midweek or Saturday clubs

These are often very effective in attracting children who are unused to church. What happens at a club needs to be right for the group and will depend to some extent on when the club runs. Running a club with some Bible-based activities could be the next stage on from a 'special interest' club. One church that tried out some new material for Scripture Union said, 'We didn't think we could do spiritual things at our midweek club, but it works!' The leader of a children's club in Liverpool says, 'We want to give the children the best hour of their week.' What a great aim!

So here are some 'top tips' for midweek clubs. (Check out the tips for holiday clubs too.)

• Make the room that you use look fun and welcoming, as you might for a themed holiday club. Use a few very simple 'props' or a backdrop that is easily set out.

• If you meet straight after school, some will be tired and may want to sit quietly while others need to 'let off steam' after their day. Begin with activities that allow the children to do either of these. They will probably appreciate a drink and snack, served in a fun way.

• Put the emphasis on fun and try to avoid puzzle sheets or activities that have a 'school' feel to them. This club needs to be very different from school.

• Maximise the opportunity. Talk with the children as much as possible. Chat when they first arrive, about their day or the things they are doing later in the week. Think in advance how to chat about the

Bible passage that you use. Talk appropriately about how following Jesus makes a difference to you or how it has helped you this week.

● Help them to read the Bible. Teach them how to find books, chapters and verses, to use the index and to understand why we do not necessarily begin at page 1!

● In time, teach them to read the Bible on their own and to ask themselves questions about the passage like 'What does it tell me about God?' Introduce them to Bible reading notes such as *Join In*, *Jump On* or *Snapshots*, (Scripture Union).

● Some churches have made it part of their club strategy to visit children at home regularly, with great success. Make sure that parents know if this is to happen, that they agree to it, and that you only go in the house if they are there.

● If you have problems recruiting leaders, run the club in six-week blocks, instead of all year.

● If numbers are down in the summer term, try a different format – meet in the local park or fix some special events. If numbers are really poor, pause the club to restart in the autumn.

You will find more about midweek clubs and programmes to run such clubs on the eyelevel website: www.scriptureunion.org.uk/eyelevel

Larger gatherings
Children often love the buzz that comes from bigger gatherings where

lots of churches or Christians work together to put on special events. It is more like Saturday morning children's TV than a regular club. A programme like this usually requires a huge amount of time, effort and people in planning, preparing and presenting, and may also require a lot of technology in order to make it exciting and different. It is even more important to be clear and careful with language and concepts used to explain the Bible than in a small group, because there can be less opportunity to talk with individual children. Such events reflect lots of the fun and excitement of following Jesus and remind children that they are not alone in their interest in him.

Kidz Klubs, based on the New York 'Metro Ministries' model, are a particular type of weekly Christian club, sometimes run as a local event, drawing in children from a much wider area. In some places over 800 children are bussed in to the club!

The Max is a Bristol-based two-hour event for children from local primary school Christian groups and their friends. It is held early on a Saturday evening once a term. Around 100 children come to a fun-filled, fast-action event that uses drama, games, songs, video clips and Bible stories. See www.scriptureunion.org.uk/eyelevel and look for schools@eye level–The Max

In Leeds, X:site brings together children from a range of churches for a special event every two months.

Community

One of the key places where Christians should be found is being involved in their local community. While we may hope, pray and work for the church to be at the hub of the community, it may not feel as though that is the case to those who are unconnected with it. We need to be involved there as much as possible. What you can do will depend on where you live and what is needed, but look for openings and be ready to offer when help is needed. We may even have to step back from some church roles in order to do this, but it is so important if we are to make a difference!

Could your church organise a walking bus for school children; provide escorts on rural school buses to talk with the children; set up a toy library; encourage people to become school governors; get involved in a secular holiday club, summer fair, fair trade week, community cafés, helplines, child bereavement support, football clubs? Then there are the many things you can do with adults which build links into the community that have a knock-on effect on children.

Work out what the need is and see how you can meet it!

Telling children about Jesus

At what stage do you start to talk about Jesus and where do you begin? Much will depend on what you are doing, whether you are involved in activity-based or Bible-based work and on the children themselves. Our character should reflect Jesus, and so we will be telling them about him as soon as we meet them, but without using words.

Conversation
Every child is unique, and so is every conversation that we have with them. It would be great to give you a set of comments or questions that will take you from where you begin chatting with a child to where you say, 'Would you like to follow Jesus?' but that is impossible, of course!

So here are some 'top tips'.

- **Prayer.** Before you meet the children, ask God to be with you in the conversations, allowing you to help them, to encourage them, to recognise any openings to talk about him and to know what to say when they arise.

- **Integrity.** Be genuinely interested in the children and what they are saying. Don't just talk to them because you want to get in your bit about God. Children hate to be patronised and are quick to see through adults who are not genuine.

- **Care.** Listen very carefully to them so that you neither miss nor ignore anything important that they say. A former colleague talks of being in a school lesson where a girl had written in her news book 'On Saturday my ginny-pig died.' The teacher's only comment was, 'That is NOT how you spell guinea pig!' whereas my colleague wanted to say, 'Oh I am sorry. How long had you had him? What was his name?' While a pet's death might seem like the perfect lead in to talking about Jesus dying on the cross, be very careful. It may feel as if you are ignoring their sadness (and they will probably not listen anyway if they are upset). But genuine care and interest opens up a relationship and conversation.

- **Openness.** When appropriate, talk with the children about your own friendship with Jesus.

- **Go for it.** I once asked a group of five-year-olds with no church background what they thought God is like and I got some wonderful answers!

- **Think child.** Be guided by them and change the conversation when they have had enough. Remember Paul in Athens, who went back and talked again!

Children and the gospel message

Where do we begin to tell God's great story to children who have no background in church? There are echoes of God's story in all kinds of places. These may be a good starting place: CS Lewis Narnia books, *Dogger* by Shirley Hughes, *Guess How Much I Love You* by Sam McBratney & Anita Jeram, the film *Finding Nemo* tells of a dearly loved son who disobeys his father and is taken far away; his father goes searching for him.

None of these, nor the many other books, films or songs that contain echoes of God's story, can ever adequately explain Bible truths, but they may be a starting point.

What's God like?

What is a child's view of God when they have had little experience of church? When asked, one child announced, 'He wears a kind of a dressing gown type-thing!' If they have watched 'The Weakest Link' they may picture God as being rather like Anne Robinson, asking hard questions and showing no mercy. If they are readers of the Harry Potter stories then it may be more like Albus Dumbledore – all-seeing, all-knowing, wise and just, 'but don't mess with me!'

It may be appropriate to use images such as these as we begin to talk about what God is or is not like, but the most important step is to introduce them to Jesus who is 'the image of the invisible God' (Colossians 1:15). We must talk a lot about Jesus if children are to know what God is like. So much of the material that we use will be gospel based.

Those who are unused to church need to know the facts of the gospel narratives – about Jesus' birth, life, death, resurrection and ascension. They may know some things already, but these could be tangled up with such things as Father Christmas, or Easter bunnies that have nothing to do with the Bible accounts. Our task is to help them to know the real Jesus.

But they also need to know the meaning behind all these things – what God did through Jesus' death on the cross; what it would mean, and what difference it would make to them to follow Jesus.

Essential themes and jargon-free talk

What are the important things of the gospel to teach to children? There are various routes that we can take to help them get into the gospel story:

- It's the story of a great hero and the people who followed him
- It's a 'rescue' story
- It's a 'happy family' story
- It's a 'good defeating evil' story

Whatever else, we want children to know that it's a true story – and it contains some wonderful truths. Here's the gospel in a nutshell in the kind of language that will make sense to unchurched children.

- **Children are made by God, to be like God in character**. Like him they are made to love people, to make friends, to care about people and about the world that God has made. They have a sense of right and wrong, of fairness (just do something that favours one person or group more than another and wait for the reaction!) and other Godly characteristics.
- **Children are loved by God**. God's son Jesus, came to tell people of all ages about God and to show them, through the things he did, what God is like.
- **Jesus never did anything wrong**. Some people were jealous of him and had him killed. But three days later God brought him back to life again and, although we can't see him with our eyes or touch him with our hands, he is still alive today.
- **When Jesus went back to be with God he sent his Holy Spirit** to be with those who follow him, to help them to be more like Jesus.
- Despite being made to be like God, we are different from him. **Unlike God, we all do wrong things**, things that break God's rules. When someone breaks a rule, they are usually punished for it. When Jesus died on the cross, he did something amazing. He let himself be punished instead of us, for all the wrong things that we do. And then God did something amazing too! He made it so that if anyone believes that Jesus is his son and asks to be forgiven for the wrong things in their life, they will be forgiven by God!
- **Jesus wants us to be his friends** and to follow him as leader, forever!
- Following Jesus is great! It means asking him to help us to be more like him, and trying to do and be what pleases God. And it is a fantastic adventure!

And then what?

What happens next? What do you do when you have told them about Jesus?

DO keep the group going. Don't see telling them about Jesus as the ultimate thing and then give up on them. If they have enjoyed the activity, they will want to keep coming, so keep running the activities just the same.

DO help any who choose Jesus to grow in that. That may mean helping them to talk with their parents about it. Create ways to disciple them to maturity in faith, however long that takes.

DO keep on talking at a basic level. Saying "Yes" to Jesus does not mean that we suddenly understand everything!

DO treat children who are not ready to make that choice just the same as you did before you talked with them and the same as everyone else. Don't make them feel as if they are not valued, because they have not chosen Jesus.

DON'T give up if nobody chooses Jesus! Don't make it a big issue or keep on and on pushing it. Allow children to respond as and when they are ready. Equally, don't assume that if nobody says "Yes" the first time, that they will never be interested. Talk about it again at a later stage. It is said that the average person needs to hear the gospel message seven times for it to make sense!

Top tips for reaching unchurched children

- **Be willing** to be used by God in the ways that he chooses.
- **Be open** to be used by God even when you don't expect it.
- **Be ready** to be led by God at his pace and in his time.
- **Be led by God** so that you take the opportunities that he offers.
- **Be like God** so that those you meet see something of Jesus in you as you talk about him.
- **And be persistent.** It doesn't happen overnight, and it is rarely easy. Be prepared for it to take years, and to go on working with these children long term. But if God has begun it, he will bring it to fruition.

In the beginning... God

Olive had never planned to work with unchurched children, but God had other ideas! She found 15 children trying to steal apples in her garden and caught a couple of them, so they all came to talk and she 'dared' them to come to church that night. One took up the challenge, told the others that they had to come too, and so they all turned up at the church that evening. That was a real shock for the church! That was the start of more than 15 years of work that has influenced not just those children but the entire community where she lives.

Small children whom she thinks she has never met shout, 'Hello Olive!' as she walks down their road. Older ones come knocking at her door to chat about life, and whole families have heard something of Jesus through their children. Her more formal children's work began with fun days and then a holiday club held in her lounge. In time it developed to the point where up to 60 children would pack the tiny church hall during half-term. This is God's work. He began it and he produced the growth in it.